Spelling

Authors: **Jill Hunting**

Christine Minton

**This pack meets the national standards for adult literacy,
Writing, Word Focus E2.**

**This pack has been produced by tutors for
Suffolk County Council Community Service.**

If you would like any further information please contact:

Castle Hill Community Education Centre
Highfield Road
IPSWICH
IP1 6DG

Tel: 01473 749837

Adult and Community Learning

Castle Hill Community Education Centre
Highfield Road
Ipswich
Suffolk IP1 6DG

Telephone:
01473 749837
Facsimile:
01473 749846

Suffolk Basic Skills is jointly supported by
Suffolk Learning & Skills Council
and Suffolk County Council

Every effort has been made to trace and acknowledge ownership of
copyright. The publishers would be pleased to make suitable
arrangements with any copyright holder whom we have been unable
to trace.

**The worksheets in this pack may be copied provided they are
used solely in your institution to support learning. If you wish
to photocopy them for any other purpose, you must first gain
permission from SCC Community Education Service.**

Copyright © 2005 Suffolk County Council

Introduction

This pack comprises a collection of worksheets to help spelling at Entry Level 2.

It is divided into sections to support the examples given on page 113 of the Adult Literacy Core Curriculum.

Learners will need support with using this pack as answer pages are not given.

Pages can be used separately from the whole pack where learners need to focus on specific things.

Contents

Everyday Words

Months of the year

Write the months of the year in order, starting with January.

September   April   February   August   May
December   March   January   October
November   July   June

............*January*............

............*February*............

............*March*............

............*April*............

............*May*............

............*June*............

............*July*............

............*August*............

............*October*............

............*September*............

............*November*............

............*December*............

Find the months of the year in the square below.

2

N	O	V	E	M	B	E	R	U	N	E	J
O	S	A	D	A	C	M	J	U	L	Y	A
V	E	V	D	R	O	F	U	S	B	R	N
E	P	R	E	C	H	E	N	M	A	Y	U
M	T	I	C	H	M	B	E	R	U	E	A
B	E	L	E	U	A	R	Y	B	G	N	R
R	M	E	M	B	A	U	G	U	S	T	Y
E	B	E	B	R	M	A	P	R	I	L	M
D	E	C	E	M	B	R	A	G	S	T	B
O	R	E	R	O	C	T	O	B	E	R	Y

Fill in the missing months in the grids below.

Last month	This month	Next month
February	March	April

Last month	This month	Next month
August	October	November

Last month	This month	Next month
		September

Last month	This month	Next month
December		

Numbers 10 to 20

Write the correct numbers next to the digits.

eleven, twelve, thirteen, fourteen, fifteen, sixteen, seventeen, eighteen, nineteen, twenty

15......fifteen.....................

13......thirteen..................

20......twenty..................

18......eighteen..................

11......eleven..................

14......fourteen..................

17......seventeen

12......twelve..................

16......sixteen..................

19......nineteen.................

Fill in the missing numbers in the following.

1.   . . . . is a dozen.
2.   You come of age at . . . .
3.   You're no longer a teenager at . . . .
4.   . . . . is half thirty.
5.   "Legs . . . . "
6.   10 x 2 – 3 = ...
7.   "Sweet . . . ." .
8.   ". . . . . is a baker's dozen".
9.   Last century was the . . . . hundreds.

4

Jumbled words

Rearrange the letters in each word so they make sense.

1. uJen   ....June......
2. ebcDmere   ...decmber.
3. levwte   ....
4. yMa   ....may......
5. levnee   ....
6. gAutus   ...AuSSt....
7. raFurbey   ...Fabrurey)
8. harMc   ...mach....
9. lJyu   ...march....
10. eetorfun   ....July.....
11. netywt   ....
12. feetinf   ...feeth....

Write today's date on the line below.

....

Write your date of birth on the line below.

....

5

Names and dates

On the lines below, write a list of family and friends.
Write in the dates of their birthdays, writing the months in full.
Find out any you don't know.
You can then use the list as a reminder!

Name	**Birthday**
....	....
....	....
....	....
....	....
....	....
....	....
....	....
....	....
....	....
....	....
....	....
....	....
....	....
....	....
....	....

Vowels

Magic e

<u>Rule</u>

Adding e to certain words changes the vowel from a short sound to a long sound. e makes the vowel say its own name.

Compare the vowel sounds in the following words:

a – e words

cap	cape
man	mane
nap	nape
rap	rape
bad	bade
sham	shame
fat	fate
hat	hate

Now choose the correct word in each of these sentences:

1.   I like to have a nap/nape in the afternoons.

2.   It's a sham/shame you can't come to the party.

3.   The male lion has a man/mane.

4.   A cap/cape can keep the sun out of your eyes.

5.   I had a bad/bade night last night.

Now look at these words and compare the sounds.

i – e words

sit	site
rip	ripe
kit	kite
dim	dime
shin	shine
din	dine
fin	fine

Choose the correct word in each of these sentences:

1. These peaches aren't rip/ripe.

2. Will you help me fly my kit/kite?

3. Turn that music down! There's such a din/dine!

4. A shark's fin/fine sometimes shows above the water.

5. It's very dim/dime in here. Could you turn the light on?

6. Someone kicked his shin/shine, playing football.

o – e words

hop	hope
mop	mope
cop	cope
rod	rode
cod	code
rob	robe
not	note
dot	dote

Complete these sentences using the right word each time:

1. She tried to mop/mope the wet floor.

2. We'll have cod/code and chips for dinner.

3. The man tried to rob/robe the bank.

4. Can you cop/cope on your own?

5. Can you change a five-pound not/note?

6. He rod/rode his bike without lights.

u – e words

tub	tube
cub	cube
cut	cute
dud	dude
run	rune

Choose the right word for each of these sentences:

1. The puppies looked so cut/cute.

2. He goes for a run/rune every morning.

3. He prefers to have a shower but she prefers the bath tub/tube.

4. He found the tiger cub/cube hiding in the grass.

5. We had a hug/huge dinner last night.

6. I took the dud/dude one back to the shop.

Can you think of any other words in which the vowel changes sound when you put an e on the end? Write them below.

....

....

....

....

11

ee

teeth	sheep	feed
cheese	street	queen
meet	sleet	sheen
greet	breed	deed
sheet	creed	need

Read the words above. What do you notice about the sound of ee?

....

....

What is different about the ee in these words?

peel	wheel	steel	feel

....

....

Put words from above in these sentences, so that they make sense:

1. You . . . . to clean your . . . . every day.

2. We . . . . our pet mouse on . . . .

3. She always . . . . s me enthusiastically when

    we . . . . in the . . . .

4. I . . . . nervous behind a . . . .

ea

seat	meat	treat	preach
beach	reach	teach	please
speak	breathe	peace	clean

What sound does the ea make in the words above?

....

Underline the words in the following sentences which have the same sound and are spelt with ea:

1. The weather was lovely so we went paddling in the stream.
2. Could I have a cup of tea please?
3. I had a strange dream last night.
4. Bread is made from wheat.
5. They each had a cream tea. What a feast!
6. He took a leap off the tree stump and hit his head on a branch.

Look at these words:

bread	breakfast	health	already
weapon	spread	deaf	heaven
wealth	instead	dread	threat

What is different about the sound of ea?

....

13

© Suffolk County Council

ea

weather	heavy
health	spread
dread	head
feather	pleasure

Use the words above to complete the sentences:

1.   He takes great . . . . in doing jigsaws.

2.   He found a . . . . from a peacock's tail.

3.   She likes to . . . . jam on her toast very thickly.

4.   Good . . . . can make or break a holiday.

5.   She has a . . . . of heights.

6.   Although she liked the hat it was too big for her

     . . . .

7.   The doctor said he was in good . . . . for his age.

8.   The box was very . . . . to lift.

14

ea

Some other words using ea:

bear   pear   wear   tear

Sometimes ea has two sounds:

meal   steal   real   deal   heal

What do you notice about these words?

....

Can you think of any other words that have ea in them?
List them here. What sound does the ea make?

....

....

....

....

....

ee and ea

free	coffee	sea	tea
knee	deed	lead	cream
see	feed	read	steam
three	speed	dream	ream
agree	sheep	stream	cheap
need	asleep	each	leap
indeed	cheek	reach	meal
seem	heel	mean	steal
been	steel	deal	speak
green	wheel	eat	weak
seen	street	beat	treat
week	fleet	heat	repeat
queen	sheet	seat	defeat
meet	between	east	ease
deep	reel	please	disease
keep	sweet	easy	feast
feel	teeth	peace	breathe
feet	cheese	leave	beach
bee	cheer	reason	clean

16

ee and ea

Complete these sentences using ea and ee:

1. Do you like cr. . . .m in you coff. . . .?

2. We went to the farm to s. . . . the new sh. . . .p.

3. We had gr. . . .n b. . . .ns and l. . . .ks for t. . . . .

4. We had a p. . . .ceful day by the s. . . . .

5. We had crackers and ch. . . .se to finish our m. . . .l.

6. I had a dr. . . . m about a str. . . .m when I was asl. . . .p.

7. Too many sw. . . .ts m. . . . bad t. . . .th.

8. Shin b. . . .f makes a ch. . . .p m. . . .l.

9. After her fall, her kn. . . . was very w. . . .k.

10. The bike was fr. . . . wh. . . .ling down the str. . . .t.

11. His f. . . t f. . . .l very hot in this h. . . .t.

12. We n. . . .d to r. . . .d a gr. . . .t d. . . l to improve our spelling.

y

Short words ending in y

why	pry	by
shy	fly	try
cry	sly	my
dry	sty	thy

What sound do all the words above have in common?

....

Use the words to complete the sentences.

1. Children's stories often feature a . . . . old fox.

2. He doesn't go away on holiday because he doesn't like

   . . . . .ing.

3. It was good to have some . . . . days after all that rain.

4. Young children often ask ". . . . .".

5. I couldn't find . . . . keys anywhere.

6. They had a picnic . . . . the river.

7. She didn't talk to anyone; she's so . . . .

8. "If at first you don't succeed, ... and

   . . . . again."

9. . . . . is an old word, often used in church, meaning 'your'.

ie and igh

ie and **igh** can make the same sound as '**y**' on the last page.

ie	**igh**
lie	high
die	sigh
pie	fight
tie	might

Complete the sentences below:

1. She let out a big. . . . . as she put the book down.

2. They had apple . . . . for dessert.

3. We . . . . go out for a walk; it depends on the weather.

4. He came home with a torn shirt; he'd been in a

   . . . . after school.

5. Most men don't like having to wear a . . . .

6. We try to teach our children to tell the truth and not to

   . . . .

7. The beach is very small at . . . . tide.

8. Fewer people . . . . of cancer nowadays.

er

her	verb
herd	nerve
shepherd	serve
fern	verse
stern	person
term	kernel
herb	

er is used more often as a word ending:

letter	after
baker	number
better	super
winter	butter
supper	greater
father	later

Complete these sentences:

1. A . . . . looks after sheep.

2. It was a very cold . . . .

3. The farmer has a large . . . . of cows.

4. Next week is the half . . . . holiday.

5. He has a . . . . garden.

6. She spread some . . . . on her toast.

7. A . . . . is an action or 'doing' word.

8. A . . . . is a leafy plant found in woods and heaths.

20

© Suffolk County Council

ear

sometimes says **er**.

earn   research

earnest   hearse

learn   rehearse

learning earth

heard   earthly

unheard earthquake

early   pearl

search

Use these words to complete these sentences.

1. Even after a long . . . . they still could not find it.

2. He . . . . a very loud noise.

3. We got up . . . . this morning.

4. He did not . . . . very much in that job.

5. The . . . . shook the buildings.

6. Not every oyster will contain a . . . .

7. She went to the library to do some . . . . for her project.

8. They had to . . . . the show many times.

21

ear

Look at these words:

beard   gear   fear   hear   near   dear   clear

year   tear (falls from the eye)   smear

What sound does the ear make?

....

Now look at these words:

bear   pear   wear

tear (rip something)

What sound does the ear make?

....

Put these words under headings according to how they sound:

earth   fear   heard   pear   beard   learn

search   near   bear   wear   clear   tear (rip)

er	ear	air

22

ar

When 'r' follows a, e, i, o, u it changes the vowel to a longer sound e.g: c ā r, h ē r.

car	starch	cart	dark	lard
bar	arm	dart	hark	yard
far	farm	chart	lark	sharp
jar	harm	part	mark	harp
tar	charm	tart	park	tarnish
scar	barn	start	shark	garden
star	darn	party	spark	pardon
arch	yarn	ark	card	
march	art	bark	hard	

Complete these sentences:

1. Their new . . . . goes very fast.

2. Too much . . . . makes clothes very hard.

3. We . . . . our holidays on 1st August.

4. He has a . . . . where he cut his arm.

5. She forgot to post his birthday . . . .

6. There were sheep, cows and pigs on the . . . .

7. She bought a new . . . . of jam.

8. We went for a picnic in the . . . .

9. A . . . . is a dangerous sea creature.

10. It is . . . . at night.

11. A . . . . is a musical instrument.

12. He grew flowers and vegetables in his

. . . .

au and aw

- **au**   is usual before – nt, se, t, ce and is never a word ending.

- **aw**   is usual before l, n and can end a word.

au	**aw**
cause	claw
because	draw, drawing, drawer
pause	jaw
applause	gnaw
sauce	law, lawyer
saucer	paw
fault	raw
faulty	saw
laundry	straw, strawberry
August	outlaw
autumn	shawl
author	lawn
haunt	yawn
taunt	bawl
launch	awful
caution	awkward
auction	awe
audience	crawl

au and aw

Use **au** or **aw** to complete these words.

s h _ _ l	c _ _ t i o n
c l _ _	_ _ t u m n
s _ _ c e	l _ _ n d r y
j _ _	s t r _ _
l _ _ n c h	_ _ f u l
y _ _ n	_ _ d i e n c e

Use these words to complete the sentences:

August	because	autumn	awful	lawn
laundry	caution	outlaw	straw	paw

1.   The dog licked his . . . .

2.   She took her washing to the . . . .

3.   His birthday is in the month of . . . .

4.   Robin Hood was an . . . .

5.   The policeman let him off with a . . . .

6.   . . . . follows summer.

7.   His garden has a well cut . . . .

8.   The weather yesterday was . . . .

9.   He was late for work . . . . he overslept.

10.   The rabbit had fresh . . . . in its hutch.

25

or and oor and ore

or, oor, and ore can make the same sound as aw and au.

or	oor	ore
sport	floor	more
storm	door	store
normal	poor	score
order	moor (Yorkshire)	snore
form		

Find the words above in the grid below.

S	T	O	R	M	O	O	R	D	L	O	R
L	R	R	E	O	E	R	M	O	R	E	O
S	O	O	R	F	N	E	F	O	R	E	S
C	O	S	O	L	O	R	E	R	O	R	P
O	R	T	N	O	R	D	E	R	P	O	O
R	O	O	R	O	M	R	R	O	R	O	R
E	O	R	O	R	A	O	P	L	O	R	T
R	M	E	C	E	L	O	O	M	R	O	O
E	E	P	S	O	S	N	O	R	E	A	R
O	R	F	O	R	M	S	R	O	R	E	Z

ou and ow

- **ou**   is usually followed by nd, nt, t, r , d, se, th.
- **ow**   is usually followed by er, n, l.

ou	**ow**
bound	bow
found	brow
ground	cow
hound	how
pound	now
round	flow
around	row
house	vow
mouse	show
shout	allow
out	brown
our	crown
flour	drown, drowned
hour	down
sour	town
cloud	allowed
loud, louder, loudly	showed
south, southern	flower
mouth	power
trousers	shower
mount, mountain	tower
amount	owl
count	fowl
account	growl
country	crowd

OU and OW

Use **ou** and **OW** to complete these words:

m _ _ t h   m _ _ s e

_ _ l   g r _ _ l

s h _ _ e r   s _ _ t h

t _ _ e l   b _ _ n d

h _ _ s e   p _ _ e r

t r _ _ s e r s   w i n d _ _

f l _ _ e r   f _ _ l

f l _ _ r   p _ _ n d

c l _ _ n   a c c _ _ n t

c l _ _ d   t _ _ n

c r _ _ n   a l l _ _
h _ _ n d   f _ _ n d

OU and OW

Use these words to complete the sentences:

pound	cloud	count	crowd	trousers
stout	towel	mouth	tower	shower

1. The . . . . of London is 900 years old.

2. He bought a new pair of . . . .

3. The children can . . . . from one to twenty.

4. They have a . . . . in their bedroom.

5. All the items on the market stall cost one . . . .

6. There was a big . . . . at the football match.

7. He dried his hands on the . . . .

8. The big black . . . . brought rain.

9. The old lady was very . . . .

10. The boy put a whole cake into his . . . .

oi and oy

oi comes at the beginning or in the middle of words.
oy can come anywhere in a word.

oi	**oy**
oil	oyster
boil	boy
coil	Roy
foil	toy
soil	annoy
toil	convoy
coin	destroy
join	employ
joint	enjoy
point	royal
appoint	voyage
choice	loyal
voice	
noise	
hoist	
toilet	
exploit	
avoid	
poison	
ointment	

oi and oy

Use **oi** and **oy** to complete these words:

e m p l _ _   p _ _ s o n

a p p _ _ n t   c h _ _ c e

e m p l _ _ m e n t   p _ _ s o n e d

d i s a p p _ _ n t e d   v _ _ a g e

a p p _ _ n t m e n t   d e s t r _ _ e d

e m p l _ _ e d   a v _ _ d e d

Use these words to complete the sentences:

poison	voice	avoid	soil
destroy	enjoy	joint	boy

1. She cooked a . . . . of meat for dinner.

2. . . . . can kill.

3. The . . . . broke his leg.

4. She has a loud . . . .

5. The farmer's . . . . is fertile.

6. They will . . . . their camping holiday.

7. Colorado beetle will . . . . potato crops.

8.   The footballers could not . . . . each
other and collided.

oa ow oe

oa	ow	oe
oat	elbow	toe
coat	crow	hoe
float	flow	Joe
goat	glow	foe
throat	grow	
load	know	
road	low	
toad	below	
coal	mow	
foal	row	
loaf	slow	
moan	show	
groan	snow	
loan	stow	
oak	tow	
soak		
soap		
oath		

Complete the sentences on the next page.

1.   A cold can give you a sore . . . .

2.   He plans to . . . . some cabbages in his garden.

3.   Children seldom like . . . . and water.

4.   If you hurt your . . . . it is very painful.

5.   The man had broken down and had to . . . . his lorry.

6.   The opposite of quick is . . . .

7.   He stubbed his big . . . . on the box.

Rewrite each of these sentences using the correct word in brackets:

1.   She let out a (grown / groan) at the bad news.

2.   "(No / know), I won't go to bed!" screamed the little boy.

3.   She (rode / road) the horse well.

4.   "I don't (know / no) how to change the plug," said the man.

5.   A motorway is a long, wide (rode / road).

6.   He looked very (groan / grown) up in his suit.

oo   ew   ue

food	broom	new	blue (colour)
mood	soon	few	clue
hoof	room	dew	due
cool	loop	Jew	glue
fool	boot	pew	sue
pool	shoot	stew	true
school	moon	view	avenue
stool	spoon	blew	continue
tool	droop	drew	issue
tooth	troop	chew	value
choose	root	crew	virtue
gloom	groom	flew	pursue
afternoon		grew	rescue
		screw	statue
or		threw	tissue
		knew	Tuesday
rook	cook	newt	
brook	look	pewter	
hook	good		
foot	wood		
book	wool		

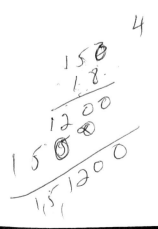

Rule: '**ue**' is usually at the end of words of more than one syllable.

35

oo ew ue

Use the words on the last page to help you choose the right word in the sentences below:

1. She <u>blew/blue</u> out the candles on the cake.
2. There was a heavy <u>dew/due</u> on the grass this morning.
3. Tomorrow is a <u>knew/new</u> day.

> Words that sound the same but are spelt differently are called homophones.

Correct the spelling mistakes in these sentences:

1. It is good to choo your food for a long time.
2. We spent the afternoon at the school swimming pewl.
3. He thrue the ball into the room.
4. I haven't a clew what's in the stew.
5. Toosday was a gluemy day.
6. Sweep the floor with the bruem.
7. You'll need some scrues and the right tewls to fix that stool.
8. The birds flue into the trap with no one to rescew them.

U

u sometimes makes the same sound as **oo** as in 'good'

       pull   full   bull

Mostly it comes in the '**ful**' that is added on to words:

       beautiful   careful   truthful

> Something added on the end of a word is called a suffix.

At other times **u** makes a different sound, as in:

       mull   cull   dull

Now complete the sentences:

1. I don't know; I'll have to . . . . it over.

2. Little boys love to . . . . little girls' hair.

3. We didn't walk through the field because there was a

   . . . . in there.

4. It was a . . . . day.

5. No more coffee, thanks. My cup's . . . .

6. I hate to watch them . . . . .ing seals, on the TV.

7. She's a very . . . . driver.

ur 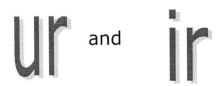 and ir

ur and **ir** give the same sound as **er**.

ur

fur (animal)	church	curse	furnish	murmur
burn	curl	urge	furniture	disturb
burst	hurl	surge	purpose	surgeon
burden	turf	urgent	purchase	Thursday
turn	nurse	further	surprise	Saturday
return	purse	surface	murder	

ir

fir	birth	birthday	
sir	third	thirteen	thirty
stir			
bird			
girl			
dirt			
shirt			
skirt			
firm			
chirp			
thirst			

ur

fur	turkey	churn
church	Thursday	burn
purse	murder	return
turn	hurt	urgent

Complete these sentences:

1. The day before Friday is . . . .

2. She had lost her . . . .

3. The runner had . . . . his leg.

4. The High Street is at the end of the road.

    . . . . left for the bus station.

5. He bought a . . . . rail ticket to London.

6. They got married at the village . . . .

39

ir

stir	bird	firm
first	shirt	thirst
dirty	skirt	girder

Complete these sentences:

1. He left his old job to start work with a new

   . . . .

2. She came . . . . in the race.

3. The car was very . . . . ; it needed a wash.

4. He bought a new white . . . .

5. She bought a bright red . . . .

6. The recipe said . . . . the sauce for five minutes.

40

ur and ir

Use **ur** and **ir** to complete these words:

b _ _ d   th _ _ t e e n

n _ _ s e   _ _ g e n t

p _ _ s e   th _ _ t y

s _ _ g e o n   S a t _ _ d a y

s k _ _ t   b _ _ r t h d a y

c h _ _ c h   m _ _ d e r

s h _ _ t   f _ _ t r e e

g _ _ l   f _ _ t h e r

f _ _ c o a t   d i s t _ _ b

p _ _ c h a s e   m _ _ m _ _

T h _ _ s d a y   b _ _ t h

t h _ _ d   r e t _ _ n

 **ur** and **ir**

Use these words to complete the sentences:

disturb	return	urgent
firm burn		dirt thirst
furnish purchase		surprise

1. An S.O.S. is always . . . .

2. On the door where the meeting was held it said,

   "Do not . . . . ".

3. They bought their car on hire . . . .

4. There was . . . . all over his clean clothes.

5. It will cost a fortune to . . . . the flat.

6. He received a nasty . . . . from the iron.

7. The birthday party was a big . . . .

8. His . . . . supplies free overalls.

9. She had to . . . . home to let the cat out.

10. A drink will quench your . . . .

ay

Use these words to complete the sentences:

play	say	may
clay	day	tray
stay	ray	gray
way	lay	pray
stray	hay	bray

1. We teach children to . . . . 'please' and 'thank you'.

2. The boys . . . . football on Saturdays.

3. "That's a lot to carry. Use a . . . .!"

4. My dog understands 'sit' and '. . . . .'.

5. What . . . . is it today?

6. Donkeys . . . .

7. The colour, grey, can also be spelt . . . .

8. I'm waiting for my hens to . . . . some eggs!

9. . . . . is dried grass.

10. Move out! You're in my . . . .

ai

ai is usually followed by **m**, **n**, or **t**
It does not come at the end of a word.

train	brain	claim
aim	braid	drain
faint	saint	taint
wait	rain	plain

What sound does the **ai** make in the words above?

....

Look at these words:

air   fair   chair

What sound does the **ai** make when it is followed by **r**?

....

(More on this on the next page.)

Now complete the sentences below:

1. During the heavy . . . . the . . . .
   overflowed.

2. We got to the station just as the . . . . was
   pulling out.

3. We had to . . . . ages for the next one.

4. He put in an insurance . . . . after the
   accident.

5. The instructions were quite . . . . and easy
   to follow.

6. There has been so much . . . . recently; the
   fields are flooded.

44

air   are   ere   ear

fair	care	there	bear
chair	scare	where	pear
hair	stare		tear
lair	rare		

The words above all have the same sound in them. What is it?

....

Can you think of any other words that have the same sound?
List them here.

....

....

....

45

Beginnings and Endings

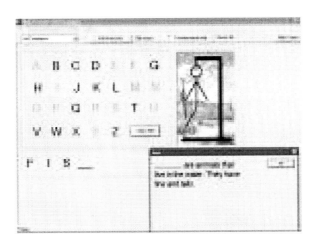

46

_s

When there is one of something, like a chair or a table for example, it is called 'singular'.

When there are two or more, it is called 'plural'.

The most common way of showing the plural is to add an **S** on the end of a word.

e.g. chair   chairs

      mug   mugs

      book   books

In the sentences below add an s to any words that you think should be in the plural.

1. Gerry thought he'd done an excellent job.

2. There were no job in the paper this week.

3. She put all the plate in the dishwasher.

4. He's thinking of buying a new computer and has looked in several shop.

5. How many biscuit did he eat?

6. The teacher were in a meeting.

7. They wanted 3 tea and 2 coffee. One of the coffee was black.

_ed

is often used at the end of a word to express the past.

e.g. I usually *walk* to work.

(Something that happens regularly uses the present tense.)

Yesterday I *walked* to work.

(Something that has already happened uses the past tense.)

Add **d** or **ed** to any words that you think should be in the past:

1. I work split shifts and I have one day off a week.

2. We play rugby last Saturday.

3. I like two sugars in my tea.

4. We didn't get any sleep last night; we talk and talk and talk.

5. Have you sign that form?

6. We're going away for the whole of August.

7. Have you finish?

8. She was so please with the flowers.

9. Try not to kick the ball into the road!

10. He couldn't remember her name.

_ ing

is often used at the ends of words following
'am', 'are', 'is', 'was', and 'were'.

e.g. He is *reading* the newspaper.

She was *sitting* outside in the sun.

> Note that when the last letter of the word is a consonant following a single vowel we double it before adding the 'ing'.
>
> hit   hitting   chat chatting   stop stopping
>
>   step stepping   cut   cutting
>
> When the last letter of the word is an 'e' we usually drop it before adding the 'ing'.
>
> please   pleasing   refuse   refusing

Add **ing** to any words you think should have it. Remember to double the last letter or cross out the e if you need to.

1.   She's go to the shops later.

2.   What were you do last night?

3.   Why are you put the salt in the fridge?

4.   Are you come round tonight?

5.   I'm have a bad day today.

6.   "I'm dream of a white Christmas."

7.   Stop fool around!

8.   She's write a letter.

un usually comes before a word to make it negative.

e.g.

happy	unhappy
do	undo
safe	unsafe
pleasant	unpleasant

Make these sentences negative by adding **un** where you think it should go:

1. She was so happy when she got home.

2. His room was incredibly tidy!

3. He is very popular at school.

4. We use leaded petrol.

5. I thought the terms were quite reasonable.

6. The teacher was very fair in the situation.

7. He eats very healthily.

8. His behaviour was most professional.

9. It was necessary to spend a lot of money on the present.

10. It's quite likely to happen.

dis_

can also come before a word to make it negative.

e.g.
appear	disappear
claim	disclaim
infect	disinfect
cover	discover

Add **dis** where you think it should go:

1. That washing powder may colour your washing.

2. Youngsters are quite respectful nowadays.

3. She's a very organised person.

4. He proved the point.

5. The old lady was pleased with the visit.

6. He taught her to mount her horse.

7. The old mill has been used for years.

8. He covered her keys, with the tea-towel.

Compound Words

Some words are made up of 2 short words.
Look at **football**. It is made up of 2 words: **foot** and **ball**.

Join the words below so that they make one word that you recognise. The first one is done for you.

tea	chair
rain	ball
motor	bow
arm	end
hand	spoon
foot	board
court	way
week	writing
key	day
birth	yard

Personal Dictionary

Use this page to write down words that you need to spell regularly. These might be names of people, names of places you visit, words you use at work or words you use for messages. Check to see if they use any of the spelling patterns you've practised in this workbook.

....

....

....

....

....

....

....

....

....

....

....

....